THE STONES
REMAIN
Megalithic Sites of Britain

D1342142

Text copyright © Kevin Crossley-Holland 1989
Photographs © Andrew Rafferty

First published in 1989 by Century Hutchinson Ltd
Brookmount House,
62–65 Chandos Place, Covent Garden
London WC2N 4NW

Century Hutchinson Australia Pty Ltd
89–91 Albion Street, Surry Hills, Sydney, NSW 2010
Australia

Century Hutchinson New Zealand Ltd
PO Box 40–086, Glenfield, Auckland 10
New Zealand

Century Hutchinson South Africa Pty Ltd
PO Box 337, Bergvlei 2012
South Africa

British Library Cataloguing in Publication Data

Crossley-Holland, Kevin.
   The stone mirrors.
   1. Great Britain. Megalithic monuments
   I. Title. II. Rafferty, Andrew
   936.1′01

   ISBN 0-7126-2206-3

Designed by Martin Lovelock

Typeset by Tradespools Ltd, Frome
Printed and bound in Great Britain by
Butler and Tanner Ltd, Frome and London

ACKNOWLEDGEMENTS

The help and support of many has gone into the making of this book.

First, my special thanks to Dina Thorpe, whose interest in the ancient sites led me to photograph them and who has in all senses paced every 'Megalithic Yard' along the way.

My thanks also to Robert Adams of the 'Old Town Arts Centre', Hemel Hempstead, who first took the work here for exhibition; to Pete Ward for sharing his photographic knowledge, and to Pete, Chris and Mike, my brothers, for their encouragement, advice and apposite remarks.

Finally, my thanks to Kevin Crossley-Holland; for a text that evokes admirably the wonder that we all feel when we confront these ancient survivals, and also for his invaluable professional advice and expertise, without which this book may never have come to fruition.

ANDREW RAFFERTY

The photographs are for 'the parents'

I am most grateful to Andy Rafferty for inviting me to write a text to accompany his superlative photographs. Both he and my father, Peter Crossley-Holland – always generous with his time and experience – read it in draft and made numerous detailed and helpful comments. I must also thank Sue Oines for tackling my handwriting and rapidly converting it into typescript.

KEVIN CROSSLEY-HOLLAND

THE STONES
REMAIN
Megalithic Sites of Britain

Photographs by
ANDREW RAFFERTY

Text by
KEVIN CROSSLEY-HOLLAND

RIDER

London · Sydney · Auckland · Johannesburg

ROUSAY

RING OF BRODGAR

CUWEEN

SKARA BRAE

STONES OF STENNESS

ONSTAN

CALLANISH + LOCH ROAG

CLAVA CAIRNS

MACHRIE MOOR

GIRDLE STANES

CAIRNHOLY + CLAUGHREID

LONG MEG

LAGGAN

MAYBURGH

CASTLERIGG

SWINSIDE

ARBOR LOW

NINE STONES

ROLLRIGHTS

MAIDEN BOWER

HAROLD'S STONES

WHITELEAF CROSS

UFFINGTON WHITE HORSE

TINKINSWOOD

WAYLAND'S SMITHY

AVEBURY

SILBURY HILL

WEST KENNET

WAMNARROW

STONEHENGE

THE GREY MARE

TRETHEVY QUOIT

MERRIVALE

MEN-AN-TOL

LANYON QUOIT

CONTENTS

THE POWER OF PLACE

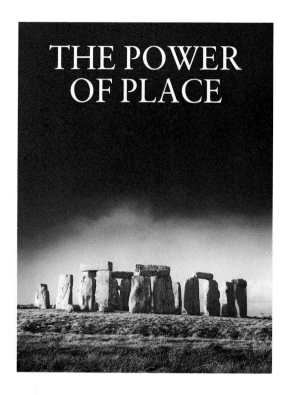

WHITELEAF HILL AND CROSS, near Princes Risborough in Buckinghamshire. The Cross was cut by Benedictine monks but there may well have been a prehistoric hill-carving on the same site. There is a Neolithic round barrow on the hill top, hidden in the beech woods, no more than a few strides from the top of the cross.

If I close my eyes and open my eyes I can see a green hill. Its curtains of beechwoods have been drawn back and its springy turf has long since been cut away to reveal a gleaming chalk cross. This cross is a bright beacon. I can see it from miles away across the shaded valley. I can see it wherever I am. And when I climb the cross to the crown of the hill I can poke amongst the molehills for potsherds and pick wild raspberries from the canes by the burial mound, then at last turn and stand where the ground plunges in front of me, and survey the world.

You and I can each think of a place, or more likely a succession of places, that matter most especially to us. Because of their beauty or some moment or period we associate with them, or because we divine in them some power to which we may have access, we visit them often in our imaginations. If anything, these personal places grow more dear to us as the years pass. In our minds they exist outside time and we see them with a kind of quickened eye and raised consciousness that is incompatible with the cut-and-thrust of the routine and humdrum. They are our demi-Edens – representing a state of innocence to which we can never fully return.

Precious and kindling in themselves, these secret places (so often associated with our early childhood) are also kernels. From them, in the grounds of our minds, there can and often does grow a greater awareness of the whole natural and man-made world in which we live our lives. We begin to sense the possibility of a continuous nourishing interplay, conducted at many levels, between the individual and the physical world.

Those of us who live in the island of Britain – the island made up of England and Scotland and Wales – inhabit, in the words of the novelist Peter Vansittart, 'an old house packed with memories'. It is no less true to think of the country as many-layered, each layer shaped by those that preceded it. The coins jingling in my trouser pocket; the laws of the land, largely submerged, that guide our exits and our entrances; the language that defines our thoughts and emotions; and the very look of the land, the green lanes, the copses, the villages – our orderly, compact yet quite spacious island: all these elements have been shaped and reshaped by succeeding generations. In each of them we can become aware of the civilizing hand of history.

When we learn to look around us in this way the everyday becomes magical. We begin to recover as adults what no child has lost: a way of seeing in which an apple is not only red or green and round, but is also a sphere, and will weep when you bite it, is speckled and freckled, and contains dark secrets. In the words of Gerard Manley Hopkins, 'There lives a dearest freshness deep down things.'

SILBURY HILL, WILTSHIRE, *built around 2700 BC, is the largest man-made mound in Europe. It is 131 feet high and covers an area of nearly five and a half acres.*

Everywhere there are mysteries. And the most ancient man-made wonders of all are the stone monuments erected by our Neolithic and Early Bronze Age ancestors between 4000 and 1500 BC – or, if it is less difficult to visualize in this way, between 140 and 240 generations ago. Little England (and smaller Scotland and Wales) are rich in these megalithic structures. Archaeologists tell us that more than a thousand chambered tombs and some 700 stone

circles have resisted the smoothing iron of wind and rain, the teeth of the plough, the grasping hands of wave upon wave of builders, always eager for good stone.

I am not speaking only for myself when I say that I cannot imagine any response more dogmatic or absurd than that of Dr Johnson when in 1773 he visited a stone circle near Inverness. 'To go and see one druidical temple', he said, 'is only to see that it is nothing for there is neither art nor power in it, and seeing one is quite enough.' On the contrary, you do not have to be an archaeologist or a latter-day astromancer to recognize that every single Neolithic and Early Bronze Age site has its own presence and that the great henges and stone circles are both aesthetically satisfying and repositories of irresistible power. For thousands of years they have held their ground. They are clothed in a wealth of traditions and stories. These ancient places are the stepping stones which lead us on a journey into times so long past, so very difficult to imagine; and at last they bring us back to ourselves, curious and ignited and empowered.

When we begin to visit megalithic monuments we may first and understandably want to ask many questions: who and how and when and why? But these stone sanctuaries do not only signify material endeavour. We may go on to find that the stones can help us, can help raise us to a level of consciousness that has nothing whatsoever to do with the factual or the causal: the world of the spirit.

WEST KENNET LONG BARROW, WILTSHIRE, overlooks the enigmatic Silbury Hill.

LAND MARKS AND LIFE MARKS

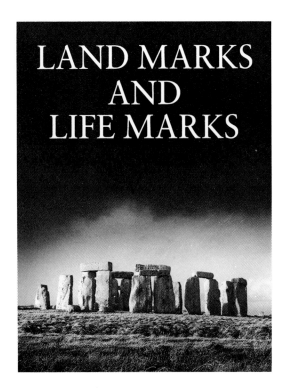

The precipitous combe known as the Manger, beneath the hill carving of the Uffington White Horse, Oxfordshire.

It is a fascinating exercise to stand in a landscape and try to visualize what it looked like even two or three hundred years ago.

If I return to my shining cross, Whiteleaf Cross in Buckinghamshire, at the foot of which I lived for most of the first sixteen years of my life, I can begin by removing certain elements: a sprawl of council houses, the railway and its slow trains running across the floor of the Vale of Aylesbury; the cement works at Chinnor. Now there are plenty of individual houses and cottages I can dispose of . . . .

When I turn to the spinneys and copses and hedges and fields I become less certain what to do. True, I have learned from W. G. Hoskins in his wonderful book, *The Making of the English Landscape*, that one can deduce the age of a hedgerow by allowing a hundred years for each species of tree and bush it contains, and know that I need subtract nothing from the landscape below me. But what about the parliamentary enclosures? Should I not split up the fields that once again look as big as the open fields of the Middle Ages and add hedge upon hedge of hawthorn? And were there not far more woodlands than survive today? And had the sycamore yet been introduced into Britain?

The subtraction is easy; we can all do it. But the addition is difficult; if we are truly to see how our landscape used to look just ten generations ago, we need the help of poets, painters, historians, archaeologists, botanists, geographers. And when we turn to prehistoric Britain we have to do without a single scrap of

written material. We must rely on scientists to piece together the vast and sometimes conflicting jigsaw of evidence and present us with facts about the lives and landscape of our distant ancestors.

The Neolithic or New Stone Age lasted from 4000 to 1800 BC (within this age the Beaker Period, named after the Beaker Folk[1] who first used copper and bronze for their tools, extends from 3000 to 1800 BC) and the Bronze Age lasted from 1800 to 800 BC. Even if we discount the first centuries of the Neolithic Age, before the earliest stone tombs were built, and the last centuries of the Bronze Age, when stone circles went out of fashion, we are still concerned with an enormous tract of time: over 2000 years.

What else was going on in the world while the spool of these ancient ages was slowly unwinding in Britain? The wheel and plough were invented in Mesopotamia and the sail in Egypt in about 3500 BC; and the first Chinese city and culture (Lung-shan) dates from about the same time. Sumerians began to use pictograph writing in about 3100 BC, and the earliest pottery to be found in the Americas, in Equador and Colombia, dates from about 3000 BC. The first great Indian civilization, in the Indus Valley, dates from about 2750 BC. Cheops built the Great Pyramid at Giza in about 2590 BC and the horse was domesticated in Central Asia at much the same time. The Minoan civilization in Crete arose in 2000 BC and was destroyed in 1450 BC. There are records of Brahma worship in India after 1450 BC and Akhenaten enforced sun worship in Egypt in 1370 BC. In 1200 BC Abraham led the Jews out of Egypt and settled in the Promised Land.

THE STONES OF STENNESS, Orkney Mainland. A stone row may once have linked the circle and henge to the Ring of Brodgar along a narrow isthmus that separates the Lochs of Harray and Stenness.

The population of Britain during the Neolithic Age, so archaeologists tell us, was a very meagre 20,000 – fewer that you will find in a single county town today. If we could step into an aeroplane and fly over the country the look of the land beneath us would bear very little resemblance at all to the present landscape. Here and there we can see open stretches of sandy heath, open wastes of moorland and the flash-and-glint of boggy marsh, but all in all the view consists of one immense, unending forest. If we look a little closer we can distinguish individual trees: a few pines, a few birches and hazels, elms and willows; above all, alder after alder, lime after lime, oak upon oak upon oak upon oak.

Now and then we can see little clusters of huts; and near these small settlements, so isolated, so separated from one another, there are signs that the forest has been deliberately fired to make room for phosphorus-rich pastures. We are looking at the very first stage in the break-up of Britain's forest cover that has proceeded apace from that time to this.

When we come down to earth again we can see what was scarcely apparent from above. Forest and open land alike are criss-crossed by a maze of paths and trails and broad tracks. Archaeologists say that these tracks, or what Christopher Taylor, in his *Roads and Tracks of Britain* (1979), calls 'zones of communication', were originally created by animals trekking between grazing grounds and were used by the nomadic hunter-fisher-gatherers of the Mesolithic (Middle Stone) Age as they moved around the country following their source of food.

AVEBURY, WILTSHIRE.
This famous stone circle is very close to West Kennet, Windmill Hill and Silbury Hill.

This carving portraying Harold's Stones can be found on a sundial in the church at Trelleck.

WAYLAND'S SMITHY, RIDGEWAY, OXFORDSHIRE.
This huge burial mound was erected in about 2820 BC on top of an earlier wooden burial chamber.

Unlike their predecessors, the Neolithic peoples learned two amazing skills: how to domesticate animals and how to cultivate crops. Instead of pursuing their prey, they could raise it and slaughter it at will; and instead of searching high and low for cereals growing wild, they could sow them and harvest them on land adjacent to their own homes. The first Neolithic peoples were nomads; at least some of the last were settled farmers.

But, of course, the need for the main trackways was as strong as ever. They were the arteries trodden by traders in absolutely essential goods: salt to eat, chert and flint axeheads and arrowheads and tools. Trade was not only local and it was by no means small-scale. Christopher Taylor says that when 400 stones found in East Anglia were examined, 'nearly sixty came from Cornwall, twenty from Wales, almost ninety from the Lake District, seven from Northern Ireland, forty-one from the Whin Sill in Northumberland, and sixteen from Charnwood Forest, Leicestershire'. The remainder had been made from indigenous East Anglian flint.

The Ridgeway, a chalk path that runs 40 miles along the escarpment of the Downs from near Avebury in Wiltshire – and may be the greatest of all Neolithic centres – to Streatley in the Thames Valley, is one of the most celebrated of Neolithic tracks. Perhaps it is not so difficult to see it as it was, occasionally punctuated by a little group of traders, flanked by newly made monuments such as the chambered long barrow known as Wayland's Smithy, constructed around 3500 BC, though the Uffington White Horse is absent:

> Before the gods that made the gods,
> Had seen their sunrise pass,
> The White Horse of the White Horse Vale
> Was cut out of the grass.

G. K. Chesterton's quatrain is evocative but untrue. This wondrous leaping horse, only seen in its full stride from the air, and so perhaps designed to be seen from above, was probably cut out of the turf between 1500 and 2000 years ago.

Nor is it difficult to see a track, like a river, leading not only from one place to another but also from one time to another. If I close my eyes and open my eyes I am back on top of Whiteleaf Cross again. I can see far beneath me two high and waving and ancient hedgerows. They flank the Icknield Way, the extension of the Ridgeway through the Chiltern Hills to Ivinghoe and on up into East Anglia. How often I have walked it! It was their track and it is mine:

> Under the moon's pale razor
> under the warm eye
> under the chamber of clouds
> under rain-dance and hail-bounce
>
> in this latitude of shadows
>
> blazing the green limbs
> foot-friend and far-reacher
> master of compounds

WEST KENNET LONG BARROW

Overseer of Epona and the fleet horses at Lambourn
the bigwigs in their hill-stations at Silbury and Chequers

keeper of Dragon Hill and the craters on the bombing range
also the quaking grass the brome grass melilot and eyebright

warden of the Og and the watercress beds and Goring Gap
the sarsens like dowdy sheep and the dowdy sheep like sarsens

custodian of the downs and brakes the strip lynchets and warrens
under the lapwing the glider's wing spring of yellow-hammers

*

And spring is the word. I can almost forget
yesterday – the sweat stain semen stain smudge
of chalk and in the hedge the sodden butts
the jagged bottle and a bloodstained rag

Here are wiry snowdrops bedded in beech mast
where wild pigs rooted. Fuses everywhere
The spindle and bryony shrug their shoulders
Birch-twigs pinken, generations within

*

A man laps at a dewpond, lays his hoar-head on his knapsack
knobby with Brandon flint. A girl in a mauve shift bares her throat
Trials riders tight-lipped burn through crimson and purple rosettes

A crocodile of the literal-minded steamy and singing
I will lift up mine eyes set their sights on the escarpment

DRAGON HILL
is part of the Uffington White Horse
complex.

Ah! the drover sleeps in a butterfly wimple – chalk-hill blues
flutter in and out of his mouth and here above the spring line
a hunter smiles as he snares such a pretty Chiltern gentian

*

It is all within me
written in chalk, and written
in your hand it is yours

whatever you may also choose . . .

From Overton to Ivinghoe
sunlight and ribs of shadows
pressing behind us and coursing
through us. We are conductors[2]

On the Orkney mainland there is an astonishing Neolithic
settlement at Skara Brae and if you have the least opportunity to
visit it you should grasp it: it is a revelation. Archaeologists are
fond of comparing the survival of this little toytown huddle of
seven stone huts – housing between thirty and forty people – to
the survival of Pompeii: the latter buried by lava in 79 BC and
Skara Brae, with its little stone alleyways and its massive refuse
heap made up of animal bones and cinders and ashes and human
and animal excrement and shells and sand, buried by a sandstorm
in about 2500 BC.

In the middle of the nineteenth century another violent storm
ripped at and stripped away the sandy turf, exposing the

SKARA BRAE,
ORKNEY MAINLAND,
had a lifespan of some 600 years. The
walls would have been rebuilt at
various intervals.

Stone carving at Onstan chambered cairn, Orkney.

SKARA BRAE
on the Orkney Mainland. The interior of a stone hut: hearth, bed and dresser.

Neolithic settlement, and the bare bones of Skara Brae have remained a matter for amazement from that day to this: hearths, stone beds doubtless once covered with a padding of aromatic mosses and herbs, overlaid with animal skins; something that resembles a stone dresser; recesses in the walls by way of cupboards; and a litter of pottery and weapons and tools and pendants and beads. There was even evidence that the storm — terrible skuthers of wind, flying debris, stinging sand — had caught the inhabitants by surprise and forced them to leave in a hurry.

At Skara Brae, as on the Ridgeway, there is a palpable sense of being in a place that has something to say to you, if only you have ears to listen, eyes to see. Standing amongst the little huts, we come closer to individuals — closer to humans with their own hopes and loves and anxieties and superstitions and their common absorption with the fabric of day-to-day life — than is possible at any other Neolithic site in Britain. Paradoxically, we are conscious both of human generality and individuality, we are aware both of change and continuity. I see Skara Brae — I hear Skara Brae — as being like a single composite sound, a soundtrack, a soundstream, stretching through time and still audible:

The place is a hiss.
The cells
and passages and womb-houses, runes of
sandstone under their turf skin,
all of them defused, bleached
into static.

Turn your back
on the usual slop and clout
and the summer blandishments
winking in the meadow.
                    Then enter,
listen …
          In the white wave
are the hiccups and polyps
and such subtle modulations
the heart decodes.
                    Nothing singular,
but in this sunken room
amongst dresser, hearth and cot,
shafted by sunlight, repossessed
after five thousand winters,
this persistent broken
singing:
          Spring and a necklace …
scattered seed … now and here
and now … all our ripening.[3]

Passageway in the Neolithic settlement at Skara Brae, Orkney Mainland. To left and right are little stone huts.

The Neolithic and Early Bronze Age peoples constructed little settlements of stone and timber, and on hilltops they threw up earthworks sometimes called causewayed camps, banks and ditches surrounding enclosures which were probably trading centres – the first precursors of the livestock and food markets in so many British towns. They erected stone chambers to honour their dead, and with great labour covered them with mounds of

pebbles or earth. All over Britain they set up huge standing stones and stone rows, and they built stone circles, potent then and, surrounded by stories, superstitions, suppositions, scarcely less potent today:

> Speak thou, whose massy strength and stature scorn
> The power of years – pre-eminent and placed
> Apart, to overlook the circle vast –
> Speak, Giant-Mother![4]

LONG MEG,
near Penrith, Cumbria. Close to this
twelve-foot standing stone are Long
Meg's daughters, a circle of fifty-nine
(and once of seventy) stones.

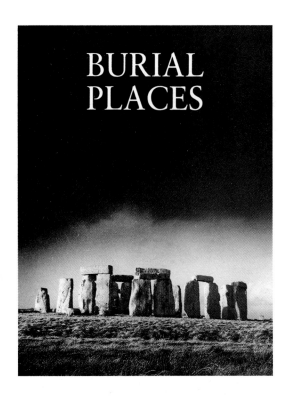

BURIAL PLACES

TREVETHY QUOIT,
north of Liskeard, is the most
impressive stone burial chamber in
Cornwall. The capstone is almost
thirteen feet long.

We have a reasonable idea of what the landscape of Britain looked like between 3000 and 5000 years ago; and, thanks to Skara Brae and to other less spectacular farmsteads and settlements such as that at Broome Heath in Norfolk, we are able to piece together a picture of the living conditions of the Neolithic and Bronze Age peoples.

Archaeologists can raise a skeleton and tell us that this middle-aged woman was crippled with arthritis or that this elderly man must have suffered appalling toothache. Look, they say, these teeth are worn down to the roots and these had abscesses. They can compare skeletons or re-embody them in plaster, and tell us that the average height of Neolithic man was 5 foot 6 inches and of Neolithic woman a couple of inches less, and that the build of the Neolithic and Bronze Age peoples was slender and lithe, like that of many Asiatic peoples today.

But all this evidence is frustrating as well as rewarding. We want to know what prehistoric man was like. It is not enough to know that the Beaker Folk ate 'land snails, pine nuts, whelks, limpets, oysters, crabs, seafish and sea birds'[5] and drank mead made from lime and meadowsweet honey. We want to know what went on in their minds. What did they talk about when they were not preoccupied with physical necessities and when the conversation moved to a higher plane – gods, spirits, the sun and the moon and the stars, life and death?

It is impossible to think of a culture, past or present, disrespectful

to its dead. The ancient Greeks laid a coin on the tongue of a corpse – payment for the ferryman Charon who would not otherwise row the deceased across the River Styx to the bright afterlife. In far-flung corners of Ireland people gather for a wake and in the presence of the corpse tell jokes and play cards and ask riddles and elbow-wrestle – and then, as the corpse leaves the place where he or she has lived, in a very few places they still keen. I have seen them and heard them. Everywhere the practices differ and everywhere (though the emphasis naturally differs from culture to culture and religion to religion) the two underlying purposes are the same: to placate the spirit of the deceased, who may resent having to leave this world and seeing his or her worldly goods pass to other people, and thus return as a ghost; and to ensure the deceased's safe passage from this world to the next.

The Neolithic peoples were no exception. Although we do not know, alas, what rituals they conducted, what songs they sang and dances they danced and instruments they played at the burial of one of their dead, and although we have no idea of what finite or infinite afterlife they believed awaited them, it is clear that they went to very considerable lengths to give at least some of their number most impressive burials and graves.

Once more I close my eyes and open my eyes .... I am waist-deep in raspberry canes, standing in the ditch encircling the round barrow on Whiteleaf Hill. In the late autumn it will fill with a great shoal of crisp blood-red and golden leaves. A group of Stone

Beech trees on Whiteleaf Hill, close to Whiteleaf Cross.

Age men dug out this ditch, two archaeologists tell us,[6] and they say that within it they built a little wooden hut, with one side open to face the rising sun. Here they strewed, within the hut and outside it, the bones of a man. Then they threw spadeful upon spadeful of earth and chalky clay over the bones, against the wooden walls, and finally right over the hut, until it was completely buried. And they cast pieces of pottery into this rising mound, some with impressions of grains of wheat in them, some incised with linear decorations; then they added charcoal and handfuls of flint flakes and the bones of many animals – deer and beaver ox and sheep – and a pin carved from one of these bones. The views of W. Johnson, in his *Byways in British Archaeology* (1912), may be speculative, but they are worth repeating:

> The original purpose of placing apparently useless pot sherds with the dead was to provide the departed tribesman with the spiritual utensils thus represented, the spirit-forms having been liberated by the breaking of the vessels. Similarly, the charcoal, the calcined pebbles, or 'pot-boilers', and few scraps of flint, would supply him with fire, first material, afterwards spiritual. Thus he had the means of making a fire, and of carrying water and hot embers.

The chambered cairn of Taversoe Tuick on the Island of Rousay, Orkney. It is unusual in being on two levels.

The burial chamber in the round barrow on Whiteleaf Hill was made of wood. But at some moment early in the Neolithic period, for some reason we will never know, people also began to construct burial chambers from stone, and these are the oldest of

all prehistoric stone structures. There are cairns; there are cists; there are quoits and cromlechs and dolmens; there are gallery graves and passage graves. And if you live in Britain or are reading this book in Britain, there is likely to be one no more than a few miles away.

The cairn (the word literally means 'heap of stones') consists of a stone tomb covered, or once covered, by a mound of pebbles or small stones. And, as one might expect, Neolithic people erected them where stone was plentiful or earth was short, largely in Wales or on the Scottish mainland, and in the Hebrides and Orkney.

The visitor to Skara Brae will find that Orkney is thick with archaeological remains – Neolithic stone circles and tombs, including the Dwarfie Stone on Hoy, the only rock-cut tomb in Britain, stand shoulder to shoulder with Viking graves, and both are flanked by the litter of the two world wars, not to mention the entire German Grand Fleet that lies at the bottom of Scapa Flow – seventy-four battleships and cruisers and destroyers scuttled by their own officers in 1919. There is a chambered cairn on Cuween Hill, and you can still stoop very low and enter it down a passage 18 feet long.

Neolithic graves almost invariably stand on their own. One does not find Neolithic graveyards or Neolithic cemeteries, although there is plenty of evidence that one burial chamber or cist sometimes accommodated more than one skeleton. Cists, indeed,

CUWEEN HILL.
Chambered cairn on the Orkney Mainland.

Detail of 'herring bone' stone wall, part of Tinkinswood tomb.

CAIRNHOLY II, looking over Kirkdale Sands.

sometimes seem to have been used as family tombs, opened and closed with some regularity over a number of generations. But back on the Scottish mainland, near Newton Stewart in Kirkcudbright, there are two superb cairns in close proximity, almost within hailing distance of one another. Cairnholy I and II are their names, and they are impressive both in themselves and for their position overlooking the waters of Wigtown Bay.

More than fifty people were buried in the cairn at Tinkinswood which is in the Dyffryn Woods near Barry in South Wales. Quite apart from its massive capstone – the vast slab which roofs the burial chamber and which weighs some 40 tons – I find this site all the more moving because something survives of the mound that once entirely covered the cairn. And here too I came across a tradition that I first heard long ago, associated also with the seat of the giant Idris near the summit of Cader Idris: that on three nights of the year, the eves of May Day and St John's Day (23 June) and midwinter, it is unwise to sleep near the cairn: anyone who does so will be struck dead, or go mad, or become a poet.

A dome of concrete has replaced the mound of shapely stones that once covered the Anglesey burial chamber of Barclodiad-y-Gawres, which means 'The Giantess's Apronful' – for this is one of countless features of the landscape and archaeological sites in Britain that we have to thank giantesses and giants for. Nor does the devil lag far behind them!

This dome covers the Neolithic burial chamber and, more

Rubbing of a cup and ring 'keyhole' design from Laggan Hill near Cairnholy. Many cup and ring carvings can be found over a wide area in South West Scotland and Northumberland.

The chambered cairn at Midhowe on the Island of Rousay contains no less than twenty-four burial compartments.

particularly, five stones incised with zigzags and spirals, and with cupmarks and concentric circles sometimes called cup-and-ring marks. Similar rock carvings have been found in the north of England (notably the Roughting Linn stone in Northumberland) and Scotland, as well as Ireland. But what do these decorations mean? Are they sundials? Or maps? Or moulds? Are they tattooists' patterns or womb symbols or bowls used to collect sacrificial blood? No less than 104 theories have been put forward at one time or another, but archaeologists find it easier to dismiss the most absurd than to agree on the most likely; the only certain thing is that many such carvings are associated with burial sites.

The quoit and the cromlech and the dolmen are one and the same thing: a stone burial chamber, consisting of large upright slabs topped with a capstone, which was once covered in a mound of earth or barrow. Taken together, they comprise much the largest group of burial monuments surviving from Neolithic Britain, and this book can do no more that hint at their distribution, variety and haunting beauty.

There is a clutch of quoits in Cornwall, some of them within easy reach of one another. Perhaps Trevethy Quoit is the most imposing. In a quiet field between Darite and Tremar, just north of Liskeard, huge standing slabs support a capstone 12 feet long. Overall, the quoit is 15 feet high. There is a hole in the capstone and a corner cut out of one of the standing stones. Why? We do not know and the liberated imagination may legitimately conjure

up all kinds of reasons.

And then, in West Penwith, you come to Lanyon Quoit, standing by the roadside between Morvah and Madron 3 miles northwest of Penzance. Its appearance is deceptive though. It collapsed in 1815 and one standing slab broke as a team of farmers tried to re-erect it in 1824; so now the capstone stands on three feet and the fourth foot lies nearby. A man on horseback can no longer pass beneath it as he could when William Borlase (author the *The Antiquities of Cornwall*) visited the site in 1769.

Better you may think, to leave well alone. Up on Mulfra Hill the fallen capstone of Mulfra Quoit leans against one of the slabs that used to support it, its feet on the ground, its head in the sky. The supporting slabs of Chun Quoit, meanwhile, seem to have caved inward, so that the mighty capstone overhangs the burial chamber; from one angle, indeed, it looks like nothing so much as a vast stone mushroom.

No more than a couple of miles from Chun Quoit, and within sight of Lanyon Quoit, stands what must be the most suggestive prehistoric monument in Cornwall: Mên-an-Tol. These three stones originally stood in a triangle, and archaeologists say that they once comprised part of a Neolithic burial chamber, the holed stone allowing access to the chamber.

The stones of Mên-an-Tol have been credited with formidable powers:

LANYON QUOIT,
near Penzance, Cornwall. What is seen today is probably a skeletal structure that was once covered with a mound of earth, long since worn away.

Naked children were passed three times through the hole and then drawn along the grass three times in a easterly direction. This was thought to cure scrofula (a form of tuberculosis) and rickets. Adults seeking relief from rheumatism, spine troubles or ague were advised to crawl through the hole nine times against the sun.[7]

The distinguished Cornish folklorist, Robert Hunt, said the holed stone had further properties: 'If two brass pins are carefully laid across each other on the top edge of the stone, any question put to the rock will be answered by the pins acquiring, through some unknown agency, a peculiar motion.'[8]

Healing powers; prophetic powers: and today, the stones of Mên-an-Tol, looking out over vast tracts of land, seem to suggest the male and female principle, fertility, the power and continuum of life itself.

It is far from uncommon for the stones of a Neolithic tomb to be rearranged or relocated, or even removed altogether. Our respect for the past and the dead has sometimes counted for less than our desire for good building stone. Thus Nine Stones, in the Peak District in Derbyshire, is all that remains of a cromlech. It consists today of just four stones. There were once six stones but never, as you might suppose, nine. When the word 'nine' is applied to a configuration of stones – Nine Stones, Nine Maidens, Nine Ladies – it is thought invariably to mean 'noon', this after the service of nones which was celebrated at three in the afternoon

MÊN-AN-TOL,
Cornwall. The three stones once
formed part of a burial chamber.
They have been moved from their
original positions.

but later advanced to midday. The tradition shared by all these stone circles and groups is that once they were dancers and were turned to stone for dancing on the Lord's Day.

One of the stones at Nine Stones is deeply grooved, as are the Devil's Arrows in North Yorkshire. Geologists discount the likelihood that these grooves are the result of weathering. As with the decorated stones, we can only guess. Those who will come closest to understanding the Neolithic past cannot rely on facts alone; they must correctly understand the facts, and then dream.

On the island of Anglesey you will find not only a pair of cromlechs – Bodowyr and Lligwy, the latter with a huge hunk of a capstone weighing about 28 tons – but also a superb passage grave at Bryn Celli Ddu, incorporating a carved stone (the original is in the National Museum of Wales and a cast has been substituted on the site) covered with a maze of zigzags. You have only to look at this tomb, with its passage into the mound still so shapely and so striking, to think of those fairytales in which the little people disappear into hills and cliff faces; such stories are surely based in part on folk memories that reach back to prehistoric times.

The passage grave of Bryn Celli Ddu was built in about 2000 BC on the site of an earlier henge (a circular precinct defined by a bank and ditch) and a circle of standing stones. This kind of juxtaposition is unusual in Britain and the reason for it is not clear, but maybe it has to do with a desire for continuity. In her

NINE STONES
on Harthill Moor, Derbyshire. The four stones once formed part of a burial chamber.

The King Stone of the Rollright Stones. Made from jurassic limestone, it has weathered badly.

THE GREY MARE AND HER COLTS,
just a mile to the north of Abbotsbury in Dorset, was once a fine long barrow.

guide to legendary Britain, *Albion*, Jennifer Westwood visits Bryn Celli Ddu and calls to mind Pope Gregory's advice to St Augustine to take over heathen temples and shrines, to encourage people to keep coming to their familiar places of worship.

Christians have indeed regularly been good at baptizing what they could not suppress. The church at Rudston near Bridlington in North Yorkshire was built within a few yards of the Rudston Monolith, at 25 feet 9 inches the tallest standing stone in Britain, and in the twelfth century a church was built in the middle of one of the Knowlton Circles in Dorset – it is in ruins today.

On the whole the prehistoric sites of England are poorly serviced or, more often, not serviced at all. The Department of the Environment takes its duties seriously, but elsewhere the vast majority of sites are at the mercy of their individual owners, and all too often one is left wishing for a modicum of on-site help, a little pamphlet or even a single descriptive sheet, as one stands in the drizzle and peers at a huddle of lichenous grey stones.

At Clava Cairns in the Highlands, 6 miles east of Inverness and no more than a mile from the battlefield of Culloden, Edward Meldrum (F.S.A. Scot.) has joined forces with a local printer to prepare just the sort of help that visitors may find really welcome: a pamphlet that first speaks lyrically of these three passage graves 'standing in their leafy glade of old trees on the haugh of the River Nairn', and then proceeds to the details.

The cairns at Clava, their passages and chambers no longer hidden under instransigent heaps of stones, are each surrounded by stone circles. Archaeologists tell us that the cairns came first and are Neolithic, while the circles were erected in the Bronze Age. There is, incidentally, very little archaeological evidence to support the idea that British stone circles were used as burial sites. The alignment of some of the Clava stones, pointing directly to the place where the sun sets at the midwinter solstice, makes it certain that, whatever other rituals were performed around or within the circles, the site was an astronomical observatory.

Back on the mainland of Orkney, and visible from the main road between Stromness and Kirkwall, stands one of the most prepossessing and atmospheric of all Neolithic tombs, the passage grave of Maes Howe. Here is a huge mound, a hillock 115 feet in diameter and 24 feet high. To turn one's back on the bright day, on sunshine or birdsong, raindrop or snowflake, and pace down the long passage into the intense silence of the dark chamber (15 feet square) in the middle of the mound is somehow to become a participant – not to theorize about but to experience time past, and to know we all share the one human journey from life to death.

The recent replacement of a chatty guide trailing an electric lightbulb on a long cable by set patter and back lights complete with dimmers is a turn for the worse, but you can still make out holes in three of the walls which open out into little burial recesses, admire the extraordinary craftsmanship of the Neolithic

Erected between 2000 and 1800 BC, Clava Cairns are within 400 yards of Culloden.

Orcadians of 2500 BC, stoop to inspect the slabs in the passageway more than 18 feet long, examine the corbelled roof .... And Maes Howe's most unexpected feature is right in front of your nose: carvings of a dragon and of a walrus and of the Midgard serpent biting on its own tail, and runic graffiti scrawled on the walls by irrepressible Norsemen who forced their way into Maes Howe in the twelfth century. 'Jerusalem-farers burst their way into Orkahowe,' one graffito reads. And one of these Vikings, Hakon, was none the poorer for visiting the grave: 'A long time ago a great treasure was hidden here. Lucky the man who finds the great hoard! Single-handed, Hakon bore treasure out of this mound.' Maes Howe was used for secret assignations too: 'Thorny got laid in here – Helgi says so.'

It is almost invariably fascinating to see how people in time long past viewed the monuments of still-earlier times: to read the Anglo-Saxon poem, *The Ruin*, in which the poet marvels at the architectural skills that went into the making of the Roman city of Bath, already in ruins; or to read in *Agricola* how the Roman historian Tacitus regarded the Celtic druidic temples the Roman invaders found in Britain; or to find in the early twelfth century our earliest historical glimpse of Stonehenge:

> Stanenges, where stones of wonderful size have been erected after the manner of doorways, so that doorway appears to have been raised upon doorway; and no-one can conceive how such great stones have been so raised aloft, or why they were built there.[9]

CAIRNHOLY I,
one of two cairns overlooking
Wigtown Bay in Kirkudbrightshire.

This, too, is one of the pleasures afforded by Maes Howe, and I know of few greater.

It is time to return to the Neolithic Ridgeway, this time in the company of Kenneth Grahame:

> ... at once it strikes you out and away from the veritable world in a splendid purposeful manner .... No villages nor homesteads tempt it aside or modify its course for a yard; should you lose the track where it is blent with the bordering turf or merged in and obliterated by criss-cross path you have only to walk straight on, taking heed of no alternative to right or left; and in a minute 'tis with you again — arisen out of the earth as it were .... Out on that almost trackless expanse of billowy Downs such a track is in some sort humanly companionable; it really seems to lead you by the hand.[10]

First we pass the chambered long barrow so curiously named after Wayland Smith (or Weland or Volundr), the Northern Vulcan, the supernatural smith remembered in Norse and Anglo-Saxon poetry. The tradition that Wayland had his smithy here, alluded to by Sir Walter Scott in *Kenilworth* and Thomas Hughes in *Tom Brown's Schooldays*, was recorded by the antiquary Francis Wise in 1738:

> At this place lived formerly an invisible Smith, and if a traveller's Horse had lost a Shoe upon the road, he had

WAYLAND'S SMITHY, OXFORDSHIRE.
Only a short distance from Uffington White Horse.

no more to do than to bring the Horse to this place with a piece of money, and leaving both there for some little time, he might come again and find the money gone, but the Horse new Shod.[11]

At the western end of the Ridgeway there is a remarkable clutch of Neolithic monuments – the multiple circles and earthworks of Avebury (see p. 101), the West Kennet Avenue (almost a hundred pairs of great standing stones each some 50 feet apart), the chambered long barrow at West Kennet, Silbury Hill . . . .

The West Kennet barrow is almost 100 yards long; the stones that make up its burial chamber, which seems to have been shared by four or five families, were lugged here not only from the nearby Marlborough Downs but from Frome 25 miles away; one capstone weighs more than 7 tons. But even as you stand and marvel at the dedication and superb engineering skills of the Neolithic people who erected this tomb, which may have been opened and closed and reopened for more than a thousand years, and which ultimately housed forty-six skeletons (some complete, some incomplete), your eye may be drawn to Silbury Hill.

Here is the most stupendous of all prehistoric mounds in Britain or anywhere else in Europe, and for once the statistics really are worth rehearsing and pondering. The mound is more than twenty times the height of a man and its base covers an area of over 5 acres. Thirty-five million baskets of rubble, passed from hand to hand by a gang of workmen, and 18 million man-hours would

AVEBURY, WILTSHIRE.
This circle of ninety-eight undressed sarsens (twenty-seven are still in place) is very much the largest in the British Isles.

have been needed to erect it. In his authoritative *Prehistoric Avebury* (1979), Aubrey Burl estimates that in about 2750 BC (the radiocarbon date of finds in the core of the mound) the local population would have numbered about 500. Discounting the aged, cripples and children, he suggests that if everyone else had 'worked for ten hours a day for two months in the early autumn, the project would have gone on for as long as a hundred and fifty years .... Even with the most concentrated and unlikely pro-gramme employing every person in the district on full-time navvying with only the aged to tend to beasts and the fields, ten years would pass before the hill was completed.'

What can possibly have induced so immense and arduous an expenditure of time and energy? Theories abound, of course. Silbury Hill has been seen as a burial mound, but Richard Atkinson's BBC-sponsored excavation there in the late 1960s was nothing like as conclusive as everyone had hoped and ended without discovery of a burial, let alone the legendary King Sil wearing golden armour and sitting on horseback (a tradition first written down by John Aubrey). It has been seen as a pyramid substitute housing the body and bones of an immigrant from Egypt, head of the astronomical observatory at Stonehenge! It has been seen as a sundial. It has been seen as an observatory (but in that case why is it situated in damp, lowlying ground?). It has been seen as an earth goddess or the womb of an earth goddess.

I have no personal theory about the purpose of Silbury Hill, but am conscious that studies of prehistoric Britain are bedevilled by

SILBURY HILL,
Wiltshire, is a huge Neolithic mound
which has yet to reveal its essential
secrets.

too many theorists obsessed by their own viewpoints. Of course anyone who is at all interested in prehistoric monuments is eager to get at the original function of Silbury Hill. But scholarship has very serious limitations, while obsession is a kind of blindness. In the end it may be more enriching to set aside this theory and that theory and see this extraordinary edifice, truly one of the world's wonders, as a kind of metaphor.

Look again at Silbury Hill, almost 5000 years old! Do you see life and do you see death? Do you see hope and do you see resignation? Do you see singularity and commonalty? Do you see continuity and do you see dislocation? How strange and how wonderful to be able to look at nothing more than a mound of earth, an earthwork with no architectural finesse though certainly the work of men who knew their soil mechanics, and to see in it a statement of the human condition.

WEST KENNET LONG BARROW, WILTSHIRE.
These sarsens were originally used to seal the burial chamber.

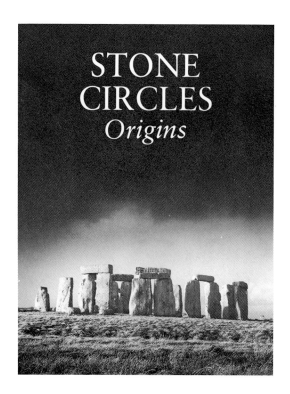

STONE CIRCLES
Origins

CAIRNHOLY II.
It is unusual for two cairns to stand in close proximity.

The ruined houses of the long-dead are always passive presences in the landscape. Stone circles, on the other hand, can take your breath away. Often immense and always open and aspiring, they proclaim just what they were: active centres – centres of practical, intellectual and spiritual activity.

The 700 surviving circles in Britain are mainly to be found in mountainous or hill country. The largest groups are in Cornwall and the Peak District, the Lake District and northeast Scotland – many north of Perth, many south of Inverness, most around Aberdeen – and the Outer Hebrides. But there are circles sprinkled throughout Wales too; there are circles in Orkney and on Dartmoor and in Wiltshire.

These monuments, together with stone rows, which were perhaps processional avenues, and individual standing stones, were erected in the late Neolithic and Early Bronze Ages, between about 2500 BC and 1500 BC. The earliest, that is to say, were put up by the same people who built the tombs discussed in the last chapter; while the latest were the work of Bronze Age farmers who migrated from continental Europe to Britain at the end of the third millennium.

It would be mistaken, though, to imagine that some great sea-change occurred in Britain around 2000 BC. The Beaker Folk had already known how to make tools from copper and bronze for a thousand years. Forest clearance proceeded at a snail's pace and many people, perhaps the majority, continued to prefer the old

nomadic to the new settled way of life. For many centuries dairy farming was to remain much more important than the growing of crops, and not until about 1400 BC did the population really begin to expand rapidly.

Until a generation ago archaeologists believed that the earliest British stone circles owed much to their counterparts in continental Europe. They pointed to such megaliths as the circular tombs in Italy or the boulder circles in Denmark, and saw them as precursors of, and models for, Long Meg and Stonehenge and Avebury. Or they postulated a common Cycladic or Egyptian origin for the various stone circles in western and northern Europe. Or, more specifically, they argued that the axe- and dagger-carvings on several of the uprights at Stonehenge proved that its builders were devotees of an axe cult (the axe being symbolic of fire, fertility and the sky god) imported from continental Europe or the Aegean.

These theories all went to the wall at the same moment when the development of radio carbon dating made it possible to give a date for the building of prehistoric monuments accurate to within a few years. Much to the surprise of most experts, it became clear that the earliest British circles had been built *before* any of their supposed European models. Stone circles, it turned out, were a British invention!

Now that the dust of this particular argument has settled it is possible to summarize the archaeological viewpoint in this way.

STONEHENGE
on Salisbury Plain, Wiltshire.
Massive sarsens from the
Marlborough Downs each weighing
up to fifty tons.

First, for some reason still to be understood, during the fifth millennium Neolithic peoples in different parts of Europe independently began to use stone as a building material for chambered tombs and subsequently for stone circles. Secondly, as there was plenty of trading contact between Britain and northwest Europe, it is highly probable that Neolithic peoples from different areas and countries exchanged views and ideas about the problems of building in stone, as well as learning something from their more civilized neighbours in Greece and the Near East. Further, it is now established that the circles in continental Europe are not only smaller than their British counterparts but, unlike the British circles, invariably enclose grave sites. And finally, the British stone circle is thought to originate in the circular earthen enclosures known as henges. As generations passed, the banks of these meeting places must have become weathered and worn; and at some point, somewhere in Britain, both to demarcate the site and to assist in astronomical observation, and maybe for other purposes, a group of Neolithic farmers decided to enhance one such henge with great slabs of stone.

CALLANISH, ISLE OF LEWIS,
in the Outer Hebrides. The ring
consists of thirteen pieces of Lewisian
gneiss.

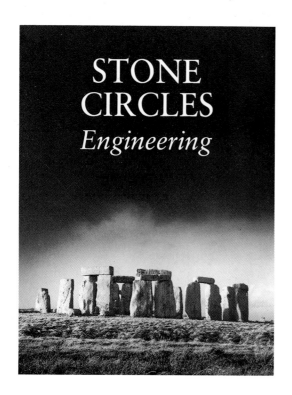

STONE CIRCLES
Engineering

The technology that enables us to put up a big building at speed is a phenomenon of the last 200 years. Like the European cathedral builders of the Middle Ages and the Indian temple builders of more than a thousand years ago, the Roman road and wall builders and the pyramid builders of ancient Egypt, the British Neolithic builders were prepared to devote years, maybe even hundreds of years, to the erection of their greatest monuments.

It is true that a few circles consist of quite 'manageable' stones, weighing hundredweights rather than tons, but many are distinguished by vast uprights visible from miles around. To have been one of a team of navvies; to have levered those stones onto specially built sledges; to have dragged them up hills and down valleys and over terrain where they might easily separate from their sledges must have been arduous and dangerous work. William Stukeley's vivid depiction of the struggle to break up a single sarsen at Avebury in the middle of the eighteenth century ironically emphasizes the lengths to which the Neolithic builders must have gone in hauling it and dressing it and setting it up:

> The barbarous massacre of a stone here with leavers and hammers, sledges and fire, is as terrible a sight as a Spanish Atto de fe. The vast cave they dig round it, the hollow under the stone like a glass-house furnace or a baker's oven, the huge chasms made through the body of the stone, the straw, the faggots, the smoak, the prongs, and the squallor of the fellows looks like a knot of devils grilling the soul of a sinner.[12]

Two of the four standing stones at Stenness on the Mainland of Orkney. They once formed part of a circle of twelve gigantic flagstones.

As one would expect, then, stone circles are to be found where there is a decent supply of stone close at hand, and there is only one instance in which it is certain that stones were transported to a circle site from a great distance.

This exception is Stonehenge, greatest and most famous of British stone circles, impressive enough in itself and grown yet taller with the innumerable traditions and speculations surrounding it. The massive sarsens – lumps of sandstone found scattered over chalk downs – at Stonehenge come from the Marlborough Downs only a few miles away. But no less than eighty-two stones, often called bluestones and weighing up to 5 tons each, come from Carn Meini in the far Prescelly (Preseli) mountains in southwest Wales.

Quite how these stones were brought to Salisbury Plain will never be known, although the theory that glaciation had a hand in it is now totally discounted. You may also be inclined to set aside Geoffrey of Monmonth's assertion in his twelfth-century *Historia Regum Britanniae (History of the Kings of Britain)* that the stones came from Africa via Ireland and that, after Utherpendragon's army, 1500 strong, were unable to move the stones with hawsers, and ropes and scaling ladders and 'every conceivable kind of mechanism', the magician Merlin raised them and spirited them by ship from Ireland to England, 'thus proving that his artistry was worth more than any brute strength'. As it is somewhat less difficult to transport stones by water than by land, the Prescelly (Preseli) bluestones, made of dolerite and rhyolite and sandstone, were in all likelihood brought down from the

CASTLERIGG
(or Carles) stone circle near Keswick in Cumbria has an unusual feature – a rectangular arrangement of stones. There are thirty-eight stones in the circle.

One of the satellite stone circles of Callanish on the Isle of Lewis, in the Outer Hebrides.

SWINSIDE,
Cumbria, circle of slate, set in the southern fells of the Lake District.

mountains to the Bristol Channel, and from there taken inland by river, always going against the stream, to some point on the River Avon a few miles from Stonehenge.

What is immensely interesting in Geoffrey Monmonth's colourful account, however, is his statement that the bluestones came from Ireland. Geoffrey was a far better fantasist than historian, and his near-contemporary William of Newburgh wrote 'that everything this man wrote about Arthur and his successors, or indeed about his predecessors from Vortigern onwards, was made up, partly by himself and partly by others, either from an inordinate love of lying, or for the sake of pleasing the Britons'[13]; but in this instance history has proved Geoffrey almost right. The stones do come from the west, and Carn Meini in the Prescelly (Preseli) Mountains lies on a major prehistoric trade route leading through south and southwest Wales to Ireland.

And why should a group of Neolithic farmers living on Salisbury Plain have gone to such trouble to secure bluestones from Carn Meini for their monument? We can only surmise that some of them had visited or passed by the mountain themselves — an important landmark for travellers, being the last the outward-bound and the first the inwardbound would see of the Welsh coast — and believed their bluestones to have magical, perhaps protective, powers. Such an idea will not seem so farfetched when we recall that Mount Olympus in Greece and Mount Ida in Crete were believed to be the homes of the gods, and that the same is true of some peaks in the Himalayas today.

And when the Marlborough Downs sarsens and Prescelly (Preseli) Mountains bluestones had at last reached Stonehenge, Aubrey Burl believes that:

> The stones were dressed, pounded with mauls, sides ground into shallow flutings, rubbed smooth, more months of work, heaved erect into their holes, stones forty tons or more, first the uprights of the trilithons, their lintel-pegs bashed from the rock, then their lintels levered plank by plank upwards on heavy hardwood cribs, then the outer circle of uprights, the inner and outer circle contained with perfect circles ... and finally, their lintels placed on top, tongued and grooved, mortised and tenoned, rebated, curved to the line of the circle.[14]

The sweat; the curses and bruises; the broken bones; the lives taken by the sudden slip or fall of a sarsen or a bluestone; the years passing; the sheer scale of the endeavour. As detail is piled upon detail we marvel not only at the technology but also at the patience and persistence of the megalith builders. For what reason, we want to know, and in what ways were stone circles so central to their lives?

AVEBURY, WILTSHIRE.
In medieval and later times, villagers
vandalized the stones.

STONE CIRCLES
Tale and Traditions

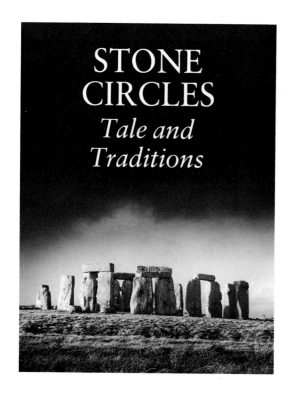

CLAVA CAIRNS
near Inverness.

There is in Cumbria, set on gently sloping ground 4 miles northeast of Penrith, a large stone circle and adjacent standing stone known as Long Meg and Her Daughters. Long Meg was a local witch and she and her coven are said to have been turned into these massive stones – the heaviest of them weighs about 28 tons – by the astrologer Michael Scott of Kelso (*c.* 1175–1230). Another tradition has it that the circle consists of Long Meg's petrified lovers, and that when she was chipped Long Meg herself once used to ooze blood.

Far south on Salisbury Plain, meanwhile, people used to steer clear of the West Kennet long barrow on the eve of the midsummer solstice because everyone knew that it was frequented by the ghost of a priest accompanied by a large white dog.

What are these traditions if not dim folk memories of the magic properties of two prehistoric sites and even of the rites once celebrated at them? All over Britain megaliths – and especially stone circles – have legends, folk tales, snatches of verse and customs associated with them. Even if we allow for the fact that many of these traditions are no more than a few hundred years old and concede that there is often no way of distinguishing the old from the new, it seems quite clear that folk beliefs have much to tell us not only about the people who perpetuated them but also about the relationship between the stones and their builders.

Let me return for a last time to my green hill at Whiteleaf. As a

very small boy I remember watching the chalk cross being cleaned by a pack of Boy Scouts. For a whole week they crawled over its surface like ants, weeding it and edging it. By the time they had finished it gleamed as it had done when the Benedictine monks of Monks Risborough first cut it out of the hill; although there is a school of thought that those monks were not the first hill carvers at Whiteleaf, but only converted a much earlier, prehistoric carving into a cross.

This whitening of the cross was no more than a dutiful mid-twentieth-century echo of the scenes described by Thomas Hughes in *The Scouring of the White Horse* (1859). At irregular intervals over more than a hundred years the White Horse at Uffington was not only picked to the bone but was the site of a great fair, complete with races, wrestling matches, cheese bowling and pig chases. In 1780 no less than 30,000 people headed for the White Horse to enjoy the fun of the fair.

Can we glimpse in these secular occasions something of the veneration in which the stone circles in Britain were once held? Did they too entertain spring-cleaning festivals? Like Whiteleaf Cross and the Uffington White Horse, stone circles were places of spiritual significance and the people who went to such great lengths to build them must also have taken care to keep them in good shape. Not to have done so might have alienated or neutralized the powers ascribed to them.

The atmospheric Rollright Stones in Oxfordshire and Warwick-

THE WHITE HORSE OF UFFINGTON
is over 120 yards long. Many Iron Age coins bear a markedly similar design.

shire (a mile south of the village of Long Compton and 5 miles northwest of Chipping Norton) consist of three separate sites – the King's Men, the Whispering Knights and the King Stone – and many traditions have gathered around them. As their names imply, these stones were long held to be human beings. A local king (in the time of local kings!) who had ambitions to conquer and rule the whole country was challenged by a witch here in these terms:

> Seven long strides more take thee,
> And if Long Compton thou canst see
> King of all England thou shalt be!

The King replied

> Stick, stock and stone,
> As King of England I shall be known!

But his ambitions were not to be fulfilled. His view of valley and village was obscured by a barrow and the witch, who resented the king trespassing on her land, had the last word:

> Because Long Compton thou canst not see,
> King of England thou shalt not be.
> Rise up stick, and stand still stone,
> For King of England thou shalt be none.
> Thee and thy men hoar stone shall be,
> And I myself an eldern tree!

The weathered limestone circle known as the King's Men which forms part of The Rollright Stones. The King's Men and The Whispering Knight's are in Oxfordshire while The King Stone, just across the road, is in Warwickshire.

The King Stone is said not only to be the haunt of fairies living nearby who dance around the stone, but its fabric was long thought to be a source of good fortune. People used to chip pieces off it for good luck and soldiers believed that to carry a chip would keep them safe in battle and give England victory.

The Rollright Stones, described by William Stukeley as 'corroded like motheaten wood by the harsh Jaws of Time', also has a tradition that may hark back to much earlier practices. It is said that you cannot count the number of the King's Men and that, in an unsuccessful attempt to do so, a baker once laid one newly baked loaf on the top of every stone he had counted. A similar story with the same result is told of Stonehenge where, in the words of Daniel Defoe, 'a baker carry'd a basket of bread, and laid a loaf upon every stone, and yet could never make out the same number twice';[15] whereas a man who laid penny loaves on the three stone circles in Cornwall together known as the Hurlers (this because they were said to have been human beings turned to stone 'for profaning the Lord's Day with hurling the ball'[16]) had more success and arrived at a definite number.

When you come across further stories of the same kind and discover that, at other sites, people have until recent times regularly poured libations of wine or blood or left offerings of barley cakes and of flowers, it is quite legitimate to wonder whether you are peering through a glass, darkly, at discontinued harvest festivals performed in the name of forgotten gods. It is pointless to try to associate single sites with individual beliefs or

ARBOR LOW,
Derbyshire. Carboniferous limestone slabs lie prostrate.

practices, but if you look at the whole body of traditions associated with stone circles you are struck immediately by recurring motifs – not only by the belief that the stones preside over the fruitfulness of the land but by the conviction that they have in their power the physical and mental health, fertility, good luck and prosperity of human beings.

Stonehenge, for instance, has long been thought to have healing powers. In his *History of the Kings of Britain* Geoffrey of Monmouth (using Merlin as a mouthpiece), after first explaining that giants carried the stones from Africa to Ireland, adds:

> Their plan was that, whenever they felt ill, baths should be prepared for them at the foot of the stones; for they used to pour water over them, and to run this water into baths in which their sick were cured .... There is not a single stone among them which hasn't some medicinal value.

In Orkney, meanwhile, two prehistoric sites have associations with fertility rites. There are four stones at Stenness, elegant blades up to 15 feet tall which once formed part of a circle of twelve stones, and until the early eighteenth century this circle was known as the Temple of the Moon, while no more than a mile away the thirty-six stones that make up the strikingly beautiful Ring of Brodgar, standing high on heathery land between two lochs, was known as the Temple of the Sun. A man and woman intending to marry used to visit each temple in turn;

THE STONES OF STENNESS, two massive blades.

Great healing powers were attributed to this stone at Mên-an-Tol.

Claughreid stone circle is only a mile to the north of the Cairnholy cairns, set on the slopes of Cairnharrow.

at the Temple of the Moon the woman prayed to the Germanic god Woden to bless her marriage and enable her to keep all her vows; then the couple walked to the Temple of the Sun where the man repeated the same prayers.

There are dozens of prehistoric monuments in Britain and Ireland that are said to ensure fertility and safe childbirth, and those interested in running them to earth will find no companion as well organized and wide ranging as *The Secret Country* by Janet and Colin Bord (1976). But, once again, such specificity has its limitations. You may rather be inclined to see stone circles in general as representative of the womb and standing stones as representative of the erect phallus. Quite often the two are to be found in juxtaposition, as is the case with the Merry Maidens stone circle and the two Pipers standing stones 4 miles southwest of Penzance in Cornwall, and in such instances the fertility imagery is all the more compelling.

Up to this point I have been concerned with what people offered up at the stones and what they believed the stones could offer them. But there is a further step to take: many stones are said to move! The Merry Maidens were dancers; so were the stones that comprise the Great Circle at Stanton Drew, one of three circles in a perfect pastoral English setting, complete with towering oaks and elms and Friesian cows, 6 miles south of Bristol; and so were the Nine Ladies on Stanton Moor, northwest of Matlock in Derbyshire. The Grey Wethers, the largest of the stone circles on Dartmoor, are still thought to go walking at sunrise, and

throughout Britain other circles are said to dance and walk and curtsy and visit nearby water for a wash or a drink.

Many of these traditions are, at any rate in their present form, Christian in origin. The stones were used in the Middle Ages as texts for sermons. Priests and monks pointed to local circles or standing stones, some of which do look uncommonly human in form, and warned that the wages of sin, such as dancing on the Sabbath, might be petrifaction. But clearly it is possible, and indeed likely, that some of these explanations overlaid much earlier memories connecting stones and movement. These memories may have reflected a belief that the stones really could move – and hence were uncountable; and they may have had to do with the ritual movements of devotees within and around the circles – movements which over the centuries became ascribed to the stones themselves.

THE RING OF BRODGAR
on the Mainland of Orkney. The diameter of the ring is almost one hundred and twenty yards. It is not only the most northerly, but also one of the most complete circles in the British Isles.

As we contemplate the enormous body of overlapping and sometimes conflicting traditions associated with prehistoric monuments in Britain, perhaps the most important point of all to grasp is just how superstitious - and I do not use the word in any pejorative sense – the prehistoric peoples were. Superstition did not stand in the margins and have to do with not walking under ladders or avoiding the number thirteen. It was a way of seeing no less real and no less significant than the rational; it was a belief in chance and coincidence and magic; it was a recognition that there are many more forms of life than the mind can perceive, and that humans are related to the physical world in far more ways than

they can understand.

Can we begin to imagine a world and a way of seeing – or should I write 'an innocence'? – in which humans enter into relationship with stones? In one of the Norse myths, Balder, the bright god of innocence and justice, is slain. In an attempt to retrieve him from the Underworld, the messengers of the gods ask every element and object to weep.

> Fire wept, iron and every other metal wept, the stones wept, earth wept, the trees wept, every kind of illness wept, all the animals wept, all the birds wept, every kind of poisonous plant wept and so did every sidling snake – just as these things weep when they are covered with rime and begin to thaw again.[17]

There was a time, before time quickened, when humans were not so much at variance with their environment as they are today. Living conditions were harsh and life was short, but people nourished the physical world around them just as they were nourished by it.

CALLANISH, ISLE OF LEWIS.
An avenue of stones and two stone rows all lead to the stones of the circle. The central stone is almost fifteen feet high.

The powerful concentration of life embodied in and expressed by stone circles can be seen as a kind of magnet. Even long after their first uses were forgotten, and after they were ruined, they continued to draw devotees and visitors and to attract tales and traditions to themselves. They continued, and indeed still continue, to be a powerful presence.

No wonder, then, that Christian teachers were suspicious of the powers of stone circles and sometimes powerless to do anything about them. In the middle of the eighteenth century ministers on the island of Lewis in the Outer Hebrides tried to stamp out the islanders' habit of visiting the wonderful standing stones at Callanish on May Day and at the midsummer solstice. But the islanders continued to go to Callanish in secret because, in the words of one contemporary, 'it would not do to neglect the stones'. According to a legend recounted in *New Light on the Stones of Callanish*,[18] 'At Midsummer sunrise, "the Shining One" was thought to walk up the avenue, heralded by a cuckoo's call.'

Between Buxton and Ashbourne in the Peak District, high above a farm where you are invited to leave a pittance in a pail on your way up, there is a prehistoric site known as Arbor Low – the name derives from the Anglo-Saxon *eorðburh-hlaw*: the earth-work mound. This consists of a Neolithic henge and, nearby, a Bronze Age burial mound known as Gib Hill. The henge's circular bank (up to 7 feet high) and ditch (up to 6 feet deep) are still impressive, and within the ditch, arranged in a circle, lie forty-two huge blocks of weathered limestone. Only one stone in the circle is still standing or, more accurately, partly standing. Archaeologists tell us that all the stones once stood, and that a few may have toppled over because their sockets, which had to be cut out of rock, were not deep enough; indeed, one eighteenth-century local said that he had seen some of the stones still standing in the 1740s.

So who went to the trouble of laying the remainder of these huge

ARBOR LOW, DERBYSHIRE.
This recumbent ring consists of fifty blocks of limestone. They are surrounded by an oval henge.

carbuncled stones? Who believed that by levelling them they could render them impotent? In all probability we can see here too the hands of anxious and zealous Christians.

MAIDEN BOWER, Bedfordshire. Originally a causewayed enclosure. Such monuments can date back to 4300 BC.

STONE CIRCLES

Function

SWINSIDE,
Cumbria is an almost perfect circle.

By now it will be apparent that there is no single or simple or certain answer to the most fascinating question of all: what were stone circles for? You can read the reports of archaeologists from dawn to dusk and you are still unlikely to be entirely satisfied ; the same is true of the calculations of astro-archaeologists, the arguments put forward by the advocates of ley lines, the theories and dreams of individuals, sometimes farsighted, sometimes muddleheaded, who have tried to tune in to the frequency of the stones. It would be better for us to approach stone circles without this jumble of received ideas going round in our heads; better simply to allow the stones to speak directly to us before turning to their would-be interpreters; but today that is scarcely possible. So the best that the honest inquirer can do is acquaint himself or herself with current thinking and use that thought as a trampoline for the imagination.

Archaeologists tell us that some of the splendid and early stone circles in Cumbria are stone counterparts to earthen henges in other parts of Britain – and that both were successors to the causewayed camps such as Windmill Hill in Wiltshire, which were probably used as meeting places for secular activities as well as sacred ceremonies.

This is to say that when we look at Cumbrian monuments such as the circle of thirty-eight stones at Castlerigg, in magnificent hilly countryside only a mile and a half east of Keswick, or the ring of fifty-five grey slate stones at Swinside, and then turn our attention to henge sites such as Broadlee and the Girdle Stones, both in

Dumfriesshire, or Arbor Low, or Avebury, we are in effect looking at one and the same thing: a spacious meeting place for Neolithic peoples who had both practical matters on their minds – such as bartering for salt or a new flint axehead – and spiritual longings to satisfy.

But at some point in the third millennium, as I have described earlier, the Neolithic people began to surmount or surround or line their earthen henges with standing stones, nowhere seen to more dramatic effect than at Avebury where, within the huge banks and ditch of the henge, originally some 55 feet from top to bottom and enclosing an area of 28 acres, stands a circle of twenty-seven sarsen stones. Once there were a hundred stones in the ring but some of them were smashed up and used to build nearby farmhouses and the cottages clustered within the circle today.

This enhancement of henges all over Britain (excepting Cumbria) with standing stones suggests one thing: that the stones fulfilled some function either poorly served or not served at all by the earthen banks and ditches. And so we come, hesitantly, to the vexed field of astro-archaeology or, if you prefer it, archaeo-astronomy.

Let me begin with the highest common factor. Archaeologists and astronomers and mathematicians and physicists would certainly be able to agree that some stone circles had some astronomical purpose. They would agree that they are oriented in much the

MAYBURGH,
Cumbria. This last surviving stone is situated in the middle of a henge.

Detail of the Lewisian gneiss used for the main Callanish complex.

CALLANISH, ISLE OF LEWIS
in the Western Isles.

manner of most churches, to face the east, and maybe even aligned to the exact point where the sun breaks the horizon at the midsummer or the midwinter solstice or at the equinoxes. They might even be able to agree that some circles are aligned to the movements both of the sun and the moon. This rather limited common ground has not been reached quickly or without argument and has tended to be overshadowed by the developments of the last twenty-five years.

In 1967 Alexander Thom – Professor Emeritus of Engineering Science at Oxford – published the results of his examination of 600 prehistoric circles, stone rows and isolated standing stones, *Megalithic Sites in Britain*. Using diagrams and mathematical tables and calculations far too complicated for most people to follow, Professor Thom argued that British stone circles were erected according to much more sophisticated principles than anyone had previously imagined, and that many were aligned not only with the movement of the sun and moon but also with Aldebaran and Pollux and Rigel and Bellatrix and other bright stars. Further, Professor Thom suggested that the circle builders all used 'a universal unit of length' measuring 2.72 feet and called by Thom the 'megalithic yard'.

Those who have looked inside *Megalithic Sites in Britain* will understand immediately how difficult it is for non-mathematicians (including archaeologists) to assess Professor Thom's arguments, and so far they have been neither fully accepted nor completely rejected. It may also occur to them that the megalithic

yard is nothing more or less than a man's average walking pace! But to my mind Aubrey Burl's trenchant analysis of one circle, Grey Croft in Cumbria, exposes the real vulnerability of Thom's calculations. Burl shows that for the sun and moon alone there are forty-six different positive alignments at Grey Croft, adding that:

> It is only after the most rigorous analysis that such alignments should be accepted for, statistically, the odds are in favour of a good celestial sight-line occurring fortuitously in almost any circle. Examining a site like Grey Croft ... there appear to be so many possible lines and so many possible targets that to discover nothing would be improbable.[19]

The implications of Professor Thom's proposals are clear and of course, they are wonderfully suggestive. Should we be thinking not of very loosely knit and self-referring tribal communities but of a society sufficiently organized by its chiefs to adopt a standard building measurement? And in place of a general astronomical awareness amongst the Neolithic peoples and a general disposition of Neolithic monuments to face or to be aligned with the rising sun, should we be thinking of master astronomers, men or women with a knowledge of the heavens wheeling over their heads and of advanced geometry? Here too Aubrey Burl stands in the way: '... had prehistoric man's prime intention been to design an astronomical monument it is unlikely that he would have constructed a circle. A line of stones for an alignment or a

One of the Stones of Stenness, Orkney.

horseshoe of pillars for calendrical computations would have been more appropriate.'

So we find ourselves, for the present at least, in a position where we can still do no better than say that stone circles, rows and standing stones served some astronomical purpose, sophisticated or simple. In either case, however, it is not a big leap to suggest that this purpose was somehow related to the deities worshipped and rituals observed at these sites. The Neolithic peoples cannot have been interested in acquiring advanced knowledge about the sun and moon and stars for its own sake but, rather, so that they could determine when to plant crops and when to celebrate festivals, and so harmonize their lives to the round of the seasons.

Anyone who has closely followed the shrinking of the daylight hours during November and then December; anyone who has made a point of watching the winter sun go down in a ball of cold flames and then felt the greater chill that immediately follows it can at least begin to imagine what the dying of the year may have meant to our ancestors. It was threatening and synonymous with death – the death of the individual and the death of the world itself; it called for supplication and propitiation. To the Neolithc and Bronze Age peoples, the sun and the moon and the stars were not inanimate but, as we can see at once from their active role in so many mythologies, living and conscious beings. They were great eyes in the sky. They could stare down at the stone monuments cast in their shape, which so often look most impressive when seen from the air, and see the human beings

MAIDEN BOWER,
BEDFORDSHIRE.
Causewayed enclosure.

congregated within them. This, I believe, suggests the kind of way in which astronomical observation, precise or imprecise, may have been translated into religious action.

In many people's minds, stone circles – and especially Stonehenge – are associated with the druids, the priests of the Iron Age Celtic people living in Britain around the time of the birth of Christ. The Roman historian Tacitus, writing in the first century AD, says that the druids conducted human sacrifices ('This inhuman people regularly shed the blood of their prisoners on their altars, and consulted their gods over the reeking bowels of men') and that their temples were in groves, while in his *Natural History* Pliny tells us that the druids conducted many of their ceremonies under oak trees, preferably (though most unusually) with mistletoe growing on them.

The association of druids and stone circles originated in the early eighteenth century. Ignoring the Classical sources, a number of antiquaries, including John Toland (*History of the Druids*, 1726) and John Aubrey and William Stukeley, took the megaliths to be druidic temples, although they differed widely in their portrayal of what the druids were actually like. Some believed them to be noble and benign seekers after truth, 'as should make our moderns asham'd, to wink in the sun-shine of learning and religion'[20]; and some, taking a lead from Tacitus and Pliny, saw them as barbaric withchdoctors perpetrating revolting sacrifices and perpetuating terrible beliefs and traditions.

LOCH ROAG STONE CIRCLE, (Callanish II) has only five stones remaining upright. It is one of ten satellite sites close to the main Callanish complex.

The occasional visits of the respectable Ancient Order of the Druids (founded in 1781) to Stonehenge, always well publicized on television, has only added to the confusion. This order claims to be in possession of arcane knowledge handed down from the time of the Celtic druids, which cannot possibly be the case. And, to underline the direct line of descent, they from time to time visit a Neolithic site completed at least a thousand years before the first Celts came to Britain in about 500 BC. It is true that the Celtic druids may have had a pre-Celtic origin and also true that the Celts did not ignore Stonehenge – Iron Age pottery has been found on the site and the area around the stones was left unworked by farmers – but there is nothing whatsoever to suggest its use as a temple.

For all this, a study of the early Celtic religion and their priests or druids has its part to play in enabling us to understand the function of the Neolithic and Early Bronze Age stone circles. There has never been a religion that did not owe much to its predecessors and it is clear that, like Christianity, the Celtic religion with its great interest in astronomy (this was recorded by Caesar), its use of water rituals and its veneration of a sun god and a mother goddess, must contain continuities and echoes of earlier beliefs and rites.

The hilltops of the West Country and the Welsh Marches are conducive to visions. In the fourteenth century William Langland went walking in the Malvern Hills and in a dream saw below him 'a fair feeld ful of folk' – the dwellers on earth who are the subject

MAYBURGH,
Cumbria. Could this have been a
prototype for other stone circles?

of *Piers Plowman*. Many a dreamer has sat on Cadbury Hill and imagined King Arthur and his knights at home in Camelot. And in 1925 Alfred Watkins published a visionary book, *The Old Straight Track*, in which he described how, sitting on a hilltop in Herefordshire, he had seen 'a network of lines, standing out like glowing wires all over the surface of the country'. Watkins went on to propose that these lines or tracks – he called them ley lines – were invariably as straight as Roman roads and that they connected strings of sun- and star-aligned ley marks, which could be a combination of stone circles, standing stones, causewayed camps, long barrows, round barrows, ponds, fords, holy wells, churches built on pre-Christian sites or the summits of high hills and mountains.

The publication of *The Old Straight Track* did not create much of a stir, but the book's time was to come in the sixties and seventies. It was taken up by an increasing number of alternative archaeologists, and before long professionals felt obliged to snub it as being a modern fairy story, based on no evidence whatosover, pointing out that in some areas of Britain there are so many prehistoric monuments and other time-hallowed sites that a straight line drawn between a couple of them several miles apart would inevitably take in one or two other sites on the way.

THE RING OF BRODGAR,
Orkney Mainland. Runic inscriptions
can still be traced on certain stones.

Devotees, on the other hand, believed that archaeologists were blinkered by their own scientific training and, in *The View over Atlantis* (1973), J. Michell asserted that 'In one moment of transcendent perception Watkin entered the magic world of

HEMEL HEMPSTEAD.

STONEHENGE,
Wiltshire.

prehistoric Britain, a world whose very existence had been forgotten.' A great throng of ley hunters sprang up and pored over maps and put on their walking boots and published their findings. Indeed, many of them are with us still.

There can be no real meeting place for archaeologists and ley hunters, let alone for those who argue that ley lines are the external symbols of underground energy currents flowing through the earth, utilized by prehistoric man, and that prehistoric monuments were storehouses used for the accumulation and dispersal of that energy.[21] The work of ley hunters (and absolutely anyone can be one) often seems overenthusiastic, or far too subjective, or just plain sloppy. But there are also things to be said for devotees of earth magic, if rather less for their findings. They alert us to the very powerful relationship that existed between prehistoric peoples and their environment and to our ancestors' animistic belief that all natural objects – every tree, every hillside, every flash of water, every stone – had a life of its own. They remind us that in our attempt to understand the Neolithic and Bronze Age peoples it is not sufficient to use our minds alone. They properly emphasize that we are concerned not only with matter but also with spirit.

Many another function has been attributed to stone circles. They have been seen as time machines, sex machines and harvest hills, and Stonehenge has been proposed both as the site of the Biblical Eden and of a 'seven-act masonic mystery play, whose performance began on 14 October 3373 BC and is still in progress';[22] and

finally, there is the school of thought that says stone circles are cast in the form of flying saucers and have served as landing pads for visitors from outer space.

Ley lines and UFOs and the like all seem to be attempts to compensate for a great absence – to deny the fact that the study of prehistoric Britain is akin to doing a jigsaw in which many of the pieces are and always will be missing. But stone circles and burial places can offer us extraordinary pleasures. We do not have to be experts to experience them. They are right under our noses and it is time now to say what they are.

THE WAMBARROWS,
Exmoor: ancient tumuli within a short distance of a stone circle, a standing stone and the ancient flagstones across the River Bark known as the Tarr Steps.

MIRRORS OF STONE

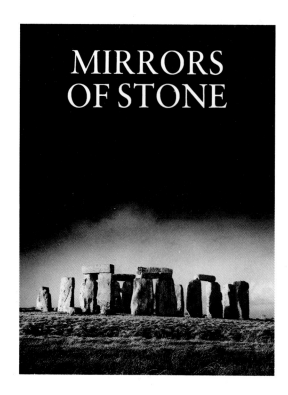

The White Esk River has cut away almost a third of the tree-ringed circle henge, known as the Girdlestanes in Dumfries and Galloway.

Some of the reasons why prehistoric circles and standing stones and tombs appeal to us so strongly are simple and obvious. Let me begin with one of them: the nature of stone. Whether one is talking of granite or dolerite or limestone or sandstone, it is stone's business to be durable. Stone is tough; stone is not easily pushed around; stone makes human life look a brief affair indeed; stones were the first ones and:

> Stones will be the last ones;
> They are earth's bones, no easy prey
> For breakers ...[23]

But while stone's density derides time, its character is endlessly fascinating. It is rough and smooth. It takes light while offering none and it is transparent, or lustrous, or even glitters with its thousand miniscule mirrors. It holds its warmth at midsummer long after the heat has gone out of the day and it is icy to touch at midwinter.

The surface of stone, moreover, tells stories of various encounters. Here the scrape of a mason's adze, there the patient craftsmanship of a skilled engraver, and everywhere the unending struggle with wind and rain. It gleams in sunlight and it seems to weep after rain. Each stone is an account of survival and suffering.

Not only the fabric but also the location of prehistoric monuments has a great attraction for many of us. A good proportion

of them are situated in places where there is little other evidence of the hand of man. When you visit the five Machrie Moor stone circles on the Isle of Arran or the nineteen boulders that make up the windswept circle at Torhouseski, near Wigtown Bay, you sense that the power of the monuments lies not only in the stones themselves but in the elemental theatre in which they are placed. And even when a village or a cluster of farm buildings stands nearby, it is usually still possible to appreciate the truths in the lie of the land and understand why the original builders placed a monument just where they did. On the whole – and, of course, Stonehenge is a serious exception – Neolithic and Early Bronze Age monuments are to be found in peaceable, places where continuity presides and gives the lie to Thomas Hardy's 'Channel Firing':

> Again the guns disturbed the hour,
> Roaring their readiness to avenge,
> As far inland as Stourton Tower,
> And Camelot, and starlit Stonehenge.

The third pleasure afforded by stone circles is that they are circles, albeit often irregular ones. Ovals would not be quite as good, and triangles or rhomboids or plain squares would be very much worse. The natural world consists of curves, not of straight lines, and the great comfort of the circle itself is that its curve is unending: it suggests the womb and the skull, the cycle of life and death and life, the rhythm of day and night, the round of the seasons and the year; earth and moon circling the sun.

One of a group of five circles on Machrie Moor on the Isle of Arran. The circle probably first consisted of eight sandstone slabs.

The close proximity, moreover, of circle and standing stone and, at Boscawen-Un on the Land's End peninsula in Cornwall, the stone's enclosure within the circle strongly suggest to me the sexual relationship and mutual dependence of male and female. Without each other they are individual and finite; taken together they express not one life or two lives but Life itself.

The mystery of stone circles and prehistoric tombs also has to do with aspiration. We pace the three stone rows at Merrivale on Dartmoor (the longest stretches almost 300 yards) and then walk clockwise round the nearby circle and are immediately conscious of effort, commitment, above all human ambition. All over Britain people lugged and tugged stones like these into position; they stood them upright; they dressed them. The megaliths may be monuments erected in the name of deities or astronomy or the dead or justice or commerce (and in all probability a combination of these), but they are also memorials to the ambition of their builders. Like Rome, they were not built in a day and their builders clearly did not mean them to perish in a day. Without cement, without mortar, simply placing stone next to stone and stone upon stone, they made quite crude structures (however complex their purposes) that awaken deep longings in us that we, too, will not die on the day we die:

And what is Time but shadows that were cast
By these storm-sculptured stones while centuries fled?
The stones remain; their stillness can outlast
The skies of history hurrying overhead.[24]

One of the three Merrivale stone rows on Dartmoor, Devon. Two of the stone rows are double and one single.

That we do not know exactly what the aspirations of the Neolithic and Early Bronze Age masons were can be frustrating, but it can also be an asset because our innocence sets our imaginations free. This is not to say that stone circles appeal because they baffle us but, rather, to assert once more the incomparable value of word and image and dream. This is the other way of seeing, the nourishing vision that no amount of fact gathering can ever achieve. It is the making real of a place to ourselves – the making personal of a place – that is indivisible from self-discovery.

As time passes and we grow older, we each want to understand rather more about our lives on this planet. We begin (or we continue) to look for meanings. When we gaze at a prehistoric circle erected 4000 or 5000 years ago we may not be sure of its function, but we know we are looking at a kind of expression – a stone understanding – of inner truth. This is why the stones draw us back. They are reflections of our own quickening search; they are monuments to the living spirit.

LOCH ROAG,
(Callanish II), on the Isle of Lewis.

NOTES

1. The Beaker Folk are named after their pottery, which typically took the form of squat, short-necked, highly decorated beakers.

2. Kevin Crossley-Holland, 'Above the Spring Line', *The Painting-Room*, 1988.

3. Kevin Crossley-Holland, 'Orkney Girls', *Waterslain*, 1986.

4. William Wordsworth, Poems Composed or Suggested During a Tour, in the Summer of 1833, XLIII.

5. D. L. Clarke, *Beaker Pottery of Great Britain and Ireland*, 1970.

6. V. G. Childe and I. F. Smith. 'Excavation of a Neolithic Barrow on Whiteleaf Hill, Bucks', *Proceedings of the Prehistoric Society*, vol. 20, 1954.

7. Janet and Colin Bord, *A Guide to Ancient Sites in Britain*, 1979.

8. Robert Hunt, *Popular Romances of the West of England*, 1865.

9. Thomas Arnold (ed.), *Henrici Archidiaconi Huntendunensis Historia Anglorum*, 1879.

10. *Pagan Papers*, 1898.

11. *Letter to Dr Mead Concerning Antiquities in Berkshire*.

12. William Stukeley, *Abury, a Temple of the Druids, with Some Others Described*, 1743.

13. *Historia Rerum Anglicarum, c.* 1185.

14. *The Stone Circles of the British Isles*, 1976.

15. *Tour through England and Wales*, 1724.

16. William Camden, *Britannia*, 1586.

17. Kevin Crossley-Holland, *The Norse Myths*, 1980.

18. Gerald Ponting and Margaret Ponting, 1984.

19. *The Stone Circles of the British Isles*, 1976.

20. William Stukeley, *Stonehenge*, 1740.

21. Janet and Colin Bord, *The Secret Country*, pp. 217–19.

22. Christopher Chippendale, *Stonehenge Complete*, 1983.

23. Kevin Crossley-Holland, 'A Place of Stones', *The Rain-Giver*, 1972.

24. Siegfried Sassoon, *The Heart's Journey*, IX, 1928.

BIBLIOGRAPHY

Books referred to in the text

John Aubrey, *Naturall Historie of Wiltshire*, 1685, ed. J. Britton, London, 1847.

Janet and Colin Bord, *A Guide to Ancient Sites in Britain*, London, 1979.

Janet and Colin Bord, *The Secret Country*. London, 1976.

William Borlase, *The Antiquities of Cornwall*, London, 1754.

Aubrey Burl, *Prehistoric Avebury*, New Haven and London, 1979.

Aubrey Burl, *The Stone Circles of the British Isles*, New Haven & London, 1976.

William Camden, *Britannia*, London, 1586.

Christopher Chippendale, *Stonehenge Complete*, London, 1983.

D. L. Clarke, *Beaker Pottery of Great Britain and Ireland*, 1970.

Kevin Crossley-Holland, *The Norse Myths*, London, 1980.

Daniel Defoe, *Tour through England and Wales*, London, 1724.

Geoffrey of Monmouth, *History of the Kings of Britain* (*c.* 1136 AD), translated by Lewis Thorpe, Harmondsworth, 1966.

Kenneth Grahame, *Pagan Papers*, 1898.

W. G. Hoskins, *The Making of the English Landscape*, London, 1955.

Thomas Hughes, *The Scouring of the White Horse*, London, 1859.

Robert Hunt, *Popular Romances of the West of England*, 1865.

W. Johnson, *Byways in British Archaeology*, Cambridge, 1912.

J. Michell, *The View over Atlantis*, London, 1973.

Gerald and Margaret Ponting, *New Light on the Stones of Callanish*, Callanish, 1984.

William Stukeley, *Abury, a Temple of the British Druids*, London, 1743.

William Stukeley, *Stonehenge: A Temple Restor'd to the British Druids*, London, 1740.

Tacitus, *On Britain and Germany*, translated by H. Mattingly, Harmondsworth, 1948.

Christopher Taylor, *Roads and Tracks of Britain*, London, 1979.

A. Thom, *Megalithic Sites in Britain*, Oxford, 1967.

John Toland, *History of the Druids*, London, 1726.

Alfred Watkins, *The Old Straight Track*, London, 1925.

Jennifer Westwood, *Albion: A Guide to Legendary Britain*, London, 1985.

Further Reading

R. J. C. Atkinson, *Stonehenge*, London, 1960.

Stan Beckensall, *Northumberland's Prehistoric Rock Carvings*, Ilkley, 1983.

N. Chadwick, *The Celts*, London, 1970.

Glyn Daniel, *The Prehistoric Chamber Tombs of England and Wales*, Cambridge, 1950.

Glyn Daniel and Paul Bahn, *Ancient Places: The Prehistoric and Celtic Sites of Britain*, London, 1987.

John Fowles, and Barry Brukoff, *The Enigma of Stonehenge*, London, 1980.

J. Hawkes, *A Guide to the Prehistoric and Roman Monuments in England and Wales*, London, 1973.

Richard Ingrams, *The Ridgeway: Europe's Oldest Road*, Oxford, 1988.

Johannes Maringer, *The Gods of Prehistoric Man*, New York, 1960.

John Michell, *Megalithomania*, London, 1982.

Ronald W. B. Morris, *The Prehistoric Rock Art of Galloway and the Isle of Man*, Poole, 1979.

Richard Muir and H. Welfare, *The National Trust Guide to Prehistoric and Roman Britain*, London, 1983.

A. Thom, *Megalithic Lunar Observations*, Oxford, 1971.

ABOUT THE AUTHORS

Born in Carlisle in 1958, Andrew Rafferty comes from a part of the country noted for its Roman associations in the shape of Hadrians Wall, and which also boasts such fine Megalithic features as Long Meg and Castlerigg. This background and his photographic interests converged in the 'Megalithic Yard' exhibition of 1985, which led directly to this book.

Kevin Crossley-Holland is a poet, writer for children, broadcaster and interpreter of the northern world. In addition to five volumes of poetry, his books include THE NORSE MYTHS, BRITISH FOLK TALES and a translation of BEOWULF, and he is the editor of THE OXFORD BOOK OF TRAVEL VERSE. He is married with two adult sons and two young daughters, and lives in Suffolk.